AUDITION PLAYBOOK

OPTIMAL PLANNING FOR ORCHESTRAL AUDITION SUCCESS

Part One: The Guide

TABLE OF CONTENTS

<u>Part Two: The Workbook</u>

FOREWORD

Dear Performers,

If you are looking to up your game in terms of a very detailed approach to audition planning and repertoire preparation, the Audition Playbook is a resource you need. Rachelle Jenkins has written a very comprehensive and thorough guide to making sure that you cover these bases during the months leading up to an important audition.

As a peak performance psychologist and someone who has helped thousands of performing artists and athletes win auditions and competitions, I believe that it is really important to have goals as well as reflect on past experiences. I appreciate the interactive nature of this book where Rachelle gives you space to do these things.

I feel very fortunate to have met and taught Rachelle during her time as a student at the Colburn School Conservatory in Los Angeles, CA. She was enrolled in my Peak Performance training class. Not only was she a driven and impressive horn student, but she was already performing often with groups including the Montreal Symphony, Los Angeles Philharmonic, Florida Orchestra, and Naples Philharmonic.

Good luck auditioning!

All the best,

Dr. Don Greene
Peak Performance Psychologist
www.winningonstage.com
Author of *Fight Your Fear and Win*, *Performance Success*, and *Audition Success*

CHANGES TO THE 2nd EDITION

If you've used a copy of the Audition Playbook before, you'll probably notice that the book you're holding looks quite a bit different! As demand for the book has grown over the past two years, so has the need to change the printing and publishing process. In doing so, certain basic formatting changes were required. Fortunately, this gave me the opportunity to explore other revisions that would change the look and effectiveness of the book. It has taken some time, but I am very happy with final product.

While many of the pages may look different in Part One, the text is almost entirely the same. There are small details added or re-worded for clarification and certain ideas have been expounded upon throughout the text. However, it is important to note that, while many additions and cosmetic changes have been made, nothing from the original book has been removed or omitted from this edition.

Part Two is entirely revamped. Each chart has been cleaned up and tweaked to reflect feedback from readers, including most notably the Weekly Practice Planning sheets. Additionally, there were previously six weeks of daily and weekly practice planning sheets printed. After surveying readers, I decided to shrink this down to four weeks. If you need more than four weeks of sheets, or if you prefer old layouts of any charts, you can download additional copies at www.auditionplaybook.com or reach out to me directly at the link below.

Thank you for your continued support in this ever-evolving project. It has been gratifying and inspiring to hear all of your stories and experiences while working through the book. As always, please feel free to reach out with any questions, comments, or suggestions. Please contact me through the website at www.auditionplaybook.com/contact/

Rachelle Jenkins
March 2020

AUDITION PLAYBOOK

OPTIMAL PLANNING FOR ORCHESTRAL AUDITION SUCCESS

Part One: The Guide

GETTING STARTED

1

What is the Audition Playbook?

The Audition Playbook is a two-part guide and workbook designed to help musicians of all instruments and levels efficiently and effectively plan and prepare for orchestra, band, and any other ensemble auditions. No matter your experience level or the level of the groups for which you are auditioning, the Audition Playbook provides the framework for you to carefully and effectively create, implement, and follow your own plan from start to finish.

Many factors go into having a successful audition and every winner will tell you about wildly different sets of tools and secrets that worked to set them apart from the pack. Every person – and every audition – is different. However, there are certain elements that tend to be universal among audition winners and, often, the most important factor is simply having a plan – a thoughtful, deliberate plan – and sticking with it.

Michael Phelps never just jumps in the pool and hopes for the best. The New England Patriots don't just casually toss the ball around in Tom Brady's backyard every weekend leading up to the Super Bowl. Every step of the way is methodically planned – from nutrition to conditioning to game day routines and beyond. In this regard, musicians preparing for auditions should be no different.

This is in no way a "one-size-fits-all" type of system and I do not endeavor to plan out your audition for you. Think of the Audition Playbook simply as the canvas upon which to design your own preparation. "Part One: The Guide" offers an overview of the the many different facets of audition preparation to consider and provides different tools, suggestions, and exercises to implement into your plan. "Part Two: The Workbook" is your personal Audition Playbook. There are no rules or requirements to the book that follows other than to have a plan, write down your plan, stick with it, and adjust accordingly.

While you will spend time planning the obvious nuts-and-bolts elements of audition preparation – your daily and weekly practice, mock auditions, travel logistics, et cetera – the Audition Playbook encourages you to prepare for the unexpected as well.

You cannot control so much of what happens on audition day – including just about every single thing that happens on the other side of the screen – but you *can* plan to account for every other possibility. What if your car breaks down on the way to the prelims? What if the proctor rushes you into the next round? What if a string breaks in your warm-up room? What if they ask for an excerpt that's not on the list? What if you don't sleep well the night before? Just giving yourself the peace of mind that you have at least *considered* the possibilities, no matter how absurd, and your possible reactions in the moment can bring a lot of comfort on audition day. Knowing that you have put in serious, measurable work on and off the instrument and seeing that work tracked in your Audition Playbook leading up to the audition can significantly boost your confidence when it's go-time.

Why did you create this?

I was a late bloomer to the horn. I gave it a try in 6th grade but abandoned it within six months. Around 11th grade, I came back around to the instrument and – somehow – ended up going to college for horn. I was very fortunate that my school, the University of Central Florida (UCF), cultivated an environment that gave me the space to make up for some of that lost time and learn how to play the instrument, while also offering numerous playing opportunities and chances to just jump in headfirst and grow. The horn was always in my hand for those four years.

When I first started at UCF, I didn't know you could actually *major* in performance... or what an "excerpt" was... or how to transpose... or that horn players even *needed* to transpose... or how people got jobs in orchestras... I had never even been to an orchestra concert! Needless to say, I had a lot of catching up to do, but UCF was a wonderful and safe place to do so.

By the time I started my master's at McGill University, I had a slightly better understanding of the orchestra world and how auditions were a huge part of that. My playing was improving, I was getting work experience in some good orchestras, and I thought I would walk out of McGill with a big job in hand.

I did not.

I advanced for the very first time during grad school in an audition for the Québec Symphony. I was *so* excited to get out first round!

But then I did not advance again for three years. Three years! It pains me even now to type that but I simply had no idea what I was doing. Admittedly, there were some big holes in my technique that needed to be sorted through, but moreover, there was a complete lack of understanding about what it takes to properly prepare for an audition and be a real contender. My preparation was lacking even when I did not realize it was lacking. I practiced the excerpts, used my metronome and tuner, recorded occasionally … so, why wasn't I advancing? And why was my performance on audition day so much worse than everything I was doing in the practice room?

After a while, I felt I must have hit a glass ceiling. I was working very hard and I knew that my playing was steadily improving but I was stuck. To say I was frustrated and discouraged would be a serious understatement. At a certain point, tired of hitting my head on the wall and expecting a different result, I stubbornly realized that it had to be more than what I was doing on the horn.

In 2015, I decided that I needed to either to go back to school and figure this out or hang it up and switch careers. As luck would have it, an opportunity presented itself at just the right time and the career change idea was put on hold. That fall, I enrolled in the Professional Studies program at The Colburn School in Los Angeles and spent my three years there working not only to fix my horn playing (which needed a lot of work) but also my approach to auditioning, performing, practicing, preparing, and thinking. I realized very quickly – with the help of my horn teacher, Andrew Bain, and performance psychologist, Dr. Don Greene – that there were so many moving parts of audition preparation that I hadn't even yet *considered*. My practice was poorly organized, I never practiced *performing*, I didn't have any strategy for mental preparation, I never committed to mock auditions … the list goes on and on.

Essentially, it all boiled down to one thing – I had no plan. In my first semester at Colburn, I advanced for the first time in years at an audition for the Montréal Symphony and I felt as though my curse was finally broken. Within the next year, I started advancing regularly, and was even making finals and super finals in auditions.

So what made the difference? The most obvious reasons are that my playing improved and that I started to develop the mental skills needed to strengthen my mind in auditions. But on top of all of that, I had a plan. For every audition, I was organized and had a plan – a plan for the weeks of preparation, a plan for the improvements to my technique, a plan for the moments on stage, a plan for how each excerpt would sound... everything.

The plan didn't always work. In fact, it often did not work. However, I took note, adjusted course, and changed the plan for the next one. I started to notice trends in my preparation and realized that many of the charts and tools I was creating for each individual audition could be compiled together in a ready-to-go workbook. With this, I could simply print out my workbook and launch straight into preparation anytime an audition was announced. Best of all, I could save my workbook with all of my notes and look back at at exactly what I did to prepare for previous auditions. This information helped to more efficiently determine which areas of my playing would need the most focus for upcoming auditions, based on clear, measurable data that I would have likely otherwise forgotten.

Around the same time, I was thinking about sports and how so much of sports psychology can relate to music. I believe this extends into our preparation for auditions in more areas than just having mental strength in performance. To have a successful audition, we have to have a solid game plan *and* an ability to execute that plan. This book functions as that plan – a playbook – in the same way that a football team has a playbook going into any game or season. It is not a restrictive plan that you must follow exactly from cover to cover or use to upend everything about your usual approach. Instead, it acts as guidance for you to create your own plan.

This seems excessive... do I really have to do everything in here?

No! But maybe for the first time, just to see which parts of the Playbook are most beneficial for you. Some may wish to follow the Playbook exactly, others may wish to pick and choose. It is up to you. The purpose of this book is not to make you follow everything here exclusively and entirely, but instead to encourage you to have a plan and to give you as many ideas as possible towards building that plan. Admittedly, as much as I love the structure and organization of many of these strategies, I can occasionally get bogged down by too much structure in my life. For some auditions, I need to do everything in the Playbook. Other times, I know I need to let the foot off the pedal a bit. I have come to this realization by going through the process many times and focusing intently and honestly on what has and hasn't worked for me. I now build my personal Audition Playbook accordingly, reflecting on what I have learned about myself in past auditions, and taking an honest look at my life in the present and the coming weeks leading up to each audition.

I believe that two of the most important factors of having a solid audition plan are flexibility and balance. If the planning here starts to feel restrictive and counterproductive to your goals, then it might be time to re-evaluate which parts of your Playbook are making you feel this way. Whatever worked for your last time might be a little too neurotic for whatever is going on in your life this time. This is normal. Give everything a fair try but be flexible and kind to yourself. The goal is to have a Playbook geared towards YOU and YOUR auditions – not to check off every box of what *should* work for everyone else.

How should I use this book?

The book is divided into two major sections. Part One is your guide to developing your own personal Audition Playbook. Part Two is your customizable Audition Playbook where you will personalize your plan and track your progress.

As you read through the instructions in Part One, begin working on the corresponding sections of your Playbook in Part Two. You may also choose simply to launch right into Part Two. As I said before, it's all up to you!

While you are encouraged to write all over the pages that follow, in speaking with many readers of the first versions of this book, I've discovered that most prefer to make photocopies of Part Two in order to keep a clean copy handy for future auditions. Others prefer to create versions of these charts by hand in their personal notebooks or create digital versions to track on their laptop or phone as they practice. Please do whatever makes you most comfortable. For supplemental PDFs, as well as Google Sheets and Excel versions of some of the charts in Part Two, please visit www.auditionplaybook.com.

If you have questions along the way, please reach out! There is an ever-growing community of Audition Playbook readers who are continuously learning, discovering, and sharing new things about their audition journeys and experiences with the book. To access the online discussion group for the Audition Playbook, please visit www.facebook.com/groups/auditionplaybook. Introduce yourself, ask questions, and share your journey with us! You can always contact me directly as well with questions, coaching requests, or to just say hello! www.auditionplaybook.com/contact/

Basic Outline of Part One: The Guide

In Chapter 2, you will see an outline of the **four phases of audition preparation**. Read through the descriptions of each phase and start working through the corresponding checklist. The amount of time you will spend in each phase depends on how many weeks you have until audition day. The Four Phases Checklist is one of the most important parts of this book and needs to be referred back to daily.

After you've figured out how many weeks there are until your audition and how much time to spend in each phase, it's time to set your **goals**. In Chapter 3, you will reflect upon past audition experiences and write out your goals for both preparation (the weeks ahead) and performance (the audition day itself). These goals will be important along the way to be able to check back in and ask yourself if you are staying true to your original intentions or needing to adjust course.

In Chapter 4, you will set your baseline by taking **initial assessments** of your technique and current knowledge of the excerpts. From here, you will develop a better idea of which parts of your technique and the repertoire list will require more of your focus and energy.

In addition to assessing your playing, you will take a brief step back and take a look at the overall picture of **balance** in your life as a whole. When do you feel you play your best, most happily, and most genuinely? In those moments, how much time are you spending dedicated to your instrument? To exercise? To spending time with friends? There is no one-size-fits-all answer, but it is important to ask yourself these questions.

Chapter 5 is the meat and potatoes of the plan. Here you will **plan your daily and weekly practicing** and track your progress along the way.

Chapter 6 focuses on the **development of performance skills**. This section is all about recording, mock auditions, rehearsing with pianists, and more.

In Chapter 7, it's Go Time. You will plan for the unplanned with **scenario planning**. You will brainstorm things that can go wrong on audition day – or that have gone wrong for you before – and decide how you will react to these scenarios in the moment. You will also develop your **audition day script**, planning the nuts and bolts of your travel, food, schedule, etc. After the audition, you will work on your **post-audition reflection** so that you're in even better shape for the next one – whenever that may be!

Following Chapter 7, you will find an extensive list of **recommended resources**. Please refer to this list as you make your way through the book and as questions arise during your preparation.

Lastly, an important note

An absolutely crucial part of audition preparation is the mental component related to centering, mental rehearsal, visualizations, self-talk, meditation, adversity training, etc. Absent here is any detailed plan regarding mental preparation – not because it is unimportant but because this area is highly personal and variable. What works for one does not work for all. I am not a psychologist and this is not a book on psychology. For further planning and exploration in this area, please refer to the recommended resources listed on pages 41-45 and at auditionplaybook.com/resources for regularly updated resources.

Additionally, it is important to remember along the way that the development of your Audition Playbook is a process – just like the development of your playing. Be patient with yourself and do not look at this book – or any resource – as the singular golden ticket to winning an audition. While your Playbook endeavors to plan for every possibility, there will always be factors for which we cannot predict.

Keep at it and enjoy the process!

PHASES OF PREPARATION

2

In the Audition Playbook, preparation is divided into four distinct phases. This is simply to ensure that all of the things you need to do on and off the instrument are done in a timely manner so that you can focus on what matters most as the audition approaches.

Each phase has its own checklist of items to accomplish within a certain time frame, ranging from logistics (e.g. booking your travel) and musical elements (e.g. making playlists of your excerpts, planning mock auditions) to checking in with your physical and mental well-being. Please feel free to make additions to your checklists. There are customizable Google Sheets and Excel versions of this checklist available online at auditionplaybook.com.

The amount of time you will spend in each phase depends on how many weeks you have until audition day. The suggested times outlined on the following pages are based on 4-week, 5-week, and 6-week plans. This tends to be the average amount of time musicians spend intensely preparing an audition, though many others spend more time than this. If you are spending more than six weeks on your preparation, feel free to adjust this timeline as you best see fit.

It can also be tricky to determine your phases when preparing more than one audition at the same time. Personally, in instances where I am preparing two auditions one or two weeks apart, I often try to keep the first two phases ("Planning" and "Early Prep") aligned to get the logistics out of the way all at once. With the "Core" and "In the Pocket" phases, I have to be more fluid and flexible, allowing myself some of the necessary rest of the final week before the first audition, while still working through some of the preparation needed for the second. In these cases, much more focused mental practice is needed to avoid overdoing it. As always, flexibility is key. The four phases exist to act as benchmarks not prison cells.

How many weeks should I take to prepare?

I don't think there is a right or wrong answer to this question. I've taken as many as eight weeks and as little as two weeks (not recommended) to prepare for auditions. I have found, for *me*, that more than six or seven weeks of intense preparation can lead to burnout and "peaking too soon." However, it's very important here to differentiate between actively and intensely preparing and casually starting to learn the list and build your technique. If there's a big audition coming up in six months and the list is huge, I will definitely start adding bits of the repertoire into my weekly practice and listening sessions as soon as possible. I treat this time as a sort of "pre-preparation" phase. I am simply building up my baseline before I switch into "audition mindset" later on. The reality is that I am indeed preparing for the audition and starting to consider the different elements of preparation during this time, but it's not my primary focus just yet. I will set a date to start ramping it up, but until then, it's just a lot of work building the baseline of my fundamentals on the horn and taking care of the concerns that will take longest to clear up. This is a mental shift more than anything.

That being said, everyone is different and every audition is different! If you prefer – and can sustain – taking many months to prepare, by all means, go for it. If you're regularly taking auditions, you're likely in great shape on the instrument, mentally strong, and your excerpts are staying fairly "in-the-pocket," so you can shorten preparation time as you see fit. If you're taking your first audition, there's likely a big learning curve ahead, so give yourself a lot of time and patience. We often have very little control over how much time we have to prepare. This is when setting clear phases and sticking to them matters most.

On the following page is an outline with brief descriptions of each phase, followed by a sample four phases planning chart (figure 2.1).

Four Phases of Preparation: Outline

1. Planning Phase

This phase focuses primarily on the logistical early-stage details, such as submitting your résumé and deposit, printing the excerpts, and setting yourself up to be fully prepared to dive into the weeks to come. You will spend the least amount of time in this phase. However, if this is your first audition, it is fine to take a little more time here to get things in order.

2. Early Preparation Phase

This phase focuses on taking initial assessments of your playing and comfort with the repertoire to set up the baseline upon which you will build, as well as ironing out further logistical details. The purpose of this phase is to know exactly where you're starting and make appropriate plans to build from there.

3. Core Preparation Phase

This phase is where you will spend the bulk of your time. This is the "heavy lifting" portion where you will do the most work on your instrument. Be mindful throughout this phase to stay balanced, healthy, and not overdo it.

4. In-the-Pocket Phase

This is the final phase prior to the audition. You will focus on getting and staying in the right headspace prior to the audition, as well as tapering your heavy practicing, in order to be in optimal physical and mental shape on the big day. At the end of this phase, after the audition, don't forget to fill out your reflection.

Four Phases of Preparation Weekly Plan – Sample (figure 2.1)

Date of my audition: December 5th

Weeks until my audition: 5 weeks

(circle one)	**PLANNING**	**EARLY**	**CORE**	**POCKET**
6 week plan	week 6 (2-3 days)	week 6 (4-5 days)	weeks 5, 4, 3, first half of 2 (3.5 weeks)	weeks 2, 1 (1.5 weeks)
(5 week plan)	week 5 (2 days)	week 5 (5 days)	weeks 4, 3, 2	week 1
4 week plan	week 4 (2 days)	week 4 (5 days)	weeks 4, 3, 2	week 1
custom				
dates:	Oct 31 – Nov 1	Nov 2 – Nov 6	Nov 7 – Nov 27	Nov 28 – Dec 4

GOALS

3

"It must be borne in mind that the tragedy of life doesn't lie in not reaching your goal. The tragedy lies in having no goal to reach."

Benjamin E. Mays

What is your goal for this audition? If you had to answer that question right this second, what would you say?

"To win?"

Of course you want to win. We all do. Who would put themselves through all of this if they didn't want to win? However, how does that singular goal play out on audition day?

The reality is, of course, that we can't control two very big factors: what the panel is looking for and who else shows up to the audition. You could play the very best audition of your career... and still not win. We can study with all the right people, learn all the repertoire, prepare and train like it's for the Olympics... and still not win. It can be a depressing and defeating journey, especially if the goal is always simply to win. Instead, we must thoughtfully and deliberately set simple, personal, specific, and *attainable* goals for both preparation and performance.

Having goals in mind for audition day and for your progress in preparation along the way can be a good guidepost as you prepare. Check in regularly. Have you strayed from your goals? Is it the goal that needs to change or your current approach? Use the Audition Goals chart (sample shown in fig. 3.1) to brainstorm your preparation and performance goals, as well as reflect upon past audition experiences. What would you like to do differently this time?

In setting your goals, sit down with a cup of coffee or tea and give yourself some time to really think about what is important. I believe setting these goals before you step out on your journey is the most important part of the process.

In the Goals chart in the Audition Playbook, there are three specific areas upon which to reflect or brainstorm. These are Past Auditions, Goals for Preparation, and Audition Day Goals.

Before we drive forward, we always need to take a glance in the rear-view mirror at what is behind us. Looking at past auditions and performances is a crucial step in making changes or building upon successes from the past. What went really well last time? What did you learn? What were you shaken by? What would you really like to improve on? You don't have to analyze every detail of every past audition but find out what jumps out to you about the recent ones that could affect this next one, for better or worse. It's good to have both some positive elements and some "needs-improvement" elements. Write it all down before you set any goals.

In the Goals for Preparation area, think about what you'd really like to achieve in the weeks ahead. This is very open-ended and you can approach this from a number of different angles. In general, this is where you set specific goals for your preparation as a whole. For example, as shown in the sample chart on page 16 (fig. 3.1), your goals for preparation might include how to divide your time between excerpts and fundamentals, strengthening a certain element of your technique or auditioning skills, or sticking to certain routines or plans.

Lastly, in the third area, Audition Day Goals, try to set a goal other than "to win!" If you've developed a specific centering technique or performance cue to focus on, that should be your goal. For many auditions I've taken, the goal has simply been to "breathe easily, blow freely" or some variation of that. Because my goal is something so simple and well-practiced, when my mind wanders on audition day, I can just bring it all back to my one singular goal, the only thing I have to focus on for the day – breathing easily and blowing freely. That's it. Everything else is outside of my goal and therefore does not need my attention.

Someone recently explained auditioning to me in a beautiful way that entirely changed my perspective on the experience. To paraphrase:

> *"Perhaps your playing was a lovely, deep green color. Your green was the greenest green to ever green! But the orchestra was looking for purple. And a purple guy showed up. He might not have played his best purple, but he was purple, so he got the job. You did not fail if your goal was to represent your green self as best as possible. You did fail if your goal was just to win."*

Audition Goals – Sample (figure 3.1)

Past Auditions Reflection

In my last audition, I didn't sleep well at all the week of the audition and it adversely affected my performance. I want to find ways to deal with this for next time. Perhaps meditation? A better routine before bed?

I utilized my time in the warm-up room really well throughout the day, but didn't stick to my plan for the final round. I was uncentered, so I need to better commit to this next time.

I didn't bring enough food to last through the day and felt pretty hungry by finals.

I tried new centering techniques that really went well and I would like to expand upon this for the next audition!

Goals for Preparation	Audition Day Goals
Stick to a daily routine as much as possible! Find out what works and write everything down. Plan my practice every night for the next day and every Sunday night for the week ahead. Record way more! Work 60% technique/40% repertoire at least for the first two weeks. Continue to develop a centering routine that works for me every time I play.	Represent my current level accurately and enjoy playing because of the work I have put in. Focus on breathing low and blowing forward! Center exactly how I have planned and practiced every day leading up. No surprises!

4

The importance of honesty and setting your baseline

To get where we're going, we've got to know where we're coming from. Just like driving a car, we need to check out mirrors and see what's behind us and all around us before moving forward.

The only way to improve upon our technique and repertoire is to be honest with ourselves about the areas which might be lacking. If my high range is worrisome and inconsistent, but my low range is super impressive, I better be working a lot more on my high range! This is common sense but, especially leading up to an audition, we can easily get wrapped up in repeatedly drilling the repertoire and finding tricks and gimmicks to get around shoddy technique. This is not sustainable and, even if it miraculously wins you the audition, it will make playing the job and getting tenure a nightmare.

Assessing your technique

In preparing for auditions, you should endeavor to keep working your technique and raising your fundamental baseline on a daily basis. Make it a priority to fill in the gaps and holes in your playing rather than drilling inefficient technique into the excerpts over and over.

If we honestly assess our baseline, we can set goals for raising it over the coming weeks leading up to the audition – and beyond! If I have assessed that my high range is weak, I am going to also identify the following: a) which excerpts on the list will most demonstrate this area of weakness, and b) any études, exercises, and pieces I can work on to improve or eliminate this vulnerability in my technique.

These assessments should not be an exercise in self-deprecation. There is a fine line between being honest and being overly critical. Try to step back and assess these areas of your technique without any internal judgement. We play how we are — but we are not our playing.

The process of honestly assessing your technique in the manner outlined below can be incredibly beneficial even without an audition on the horizon. It is especially useful when coming back from a break, an injury, or any other time you want to hit a "reset button" on your playing. An extended description of this process can be found at auditionplaybook.com/blog/reset-button.

Initial Technique Assessment

In the Initial Technique Assessment chart, list all of the elements that make up the total technique of your instrument. After you've compiled your list, honestly assess where you currently stand in each of these areas and which excerpts will showcase (for better or worse) each technique. For some, it can help to think of your favorite player, or a colleague or studio mate you admire, and compare each element of their technique to your own. (Again, do not use this as an exercise in self-deprecation). Take note of which elements will require the most immediate attention and mark those with an asterisk. In any area that is lacking, brainstorm ways to improve, such as specifically targeted études, exercises, or skills.

On the following page is a partial example of the Initial Technique Assessment as done by a horn player (fig. 4.1). Highlight the areas you are most concerned about and use your brainstorming from the "Ways to Improve" category to plan your weekly and daily practice.

Alternate Technical Assessment

Another technical assessment strategy to consider is to divide your overall technique into three categories, with the goal of eventually moving everything all the way to the right. See fig. 4.2 on the following page for a partial example.

Initial Technique Assessment – Sample (figure 4.1)

Technique	Assessment	Spotlight Excerpts	Ways to Improve
high range	improving but endurance is lacking	Brandenburg (!), Ravel Piano, Beethoven 7	etude #7, hi-flex exercise, etude #26
low range	strong; multiple tonguing articulations in this range change the sound though	Mendelssohn 3 4th horn!	multiple articulation scales
intonation	shaky on new horn	all but would be good to do a lot of slow drone work with Brahms as an exercise	drone work
soft playing	very strong	Pavane	approach from a place of ease and no tension

Alternate Technique Assessment: Sample (figure 4.2)

Parts of my technique that are shaky and could show up at the audition and eliminate me	Parts of my technique that are pretty solid and reliable	Parts of my technique that are really special that will set me apart from the rest
endurance; articulation in the low range; high range	low range; mid range; intervals; loud playing; section playing; accuracy; intonation;	liquid slurs; easy soft playing;

Assessing your repertoire

In assessing a baseline for the repertoire on the list, you can determine which excerpts are completely unfamiliar to you, which are always in your back pocket and ready to go, and which lie somewhere in the middle. With this information, you can plan your day-to-day practice accordingly, spending the earlier weeks especially more focused on the unfamiliar repertoire than the back-pocket excerpts. You will also monitor the repertoire in this way *throughout* your preparation to help you set your weekly goals. (An example of a weekly goal based off this chart would be "no 3's by the end of week 5").

The Repertoire Assessment chart is based on the system Dr. Don Greene outlines in his books *Performance Success* and *Audition Success*. In the assessment charts here, you will list each excerpt on the audition and check 3, 2, or 1, according to your current level of comfort with the piece. In this book, use the following scale:

3 = unfamiliar or needs a lot of work
2 = you know the excerpt but it needs work
1 = you nail it almost every time

Next to the rating, there is a column for you to briefly (if desired) note why the piece is rated in each column and/or how to get it to the next level.

Repertoire Assessment – Sample (figure 4.3)

Piece	3	2	1	Technical and Musical Factors
Brahms 3		x		slurs can be smoother; phrase endings choppy at breaths
Ein Heldenleben		x		articulation can be clearer in 16ths; long lines! think of playing cello
Schoenberg Chamber	x			intervals: not hearing them correctly and moving too much; my musical picture is very unclear... I need to listen and sing more!

Please note: the Repertoire Assessment should be completed in pencil, as you will adjust this chart week-by-week.

Assessing the balance in your preparation

It is important to remain mindful of how much time and focus you are dedicating to each area of your preparation.

If you are just working technique, what is happening with the repertoire? If you are just working on your instrument, what is happening with your mental game? The four components of Technique, Repertoire, Mental Training, and Performance Skills (mock auditions and recording) all work together to make up the total package that you will present on audition day. It is up to YOU to decide how to prioritize these areas. Perhaps they're exactly equal; perhaps the repertoire and technique account for 70% of the pie, and mental training and the development of performance skills only account for 30%; there's no wrong answer – it's up to you!

However, think about this before you launch into preparing. Once you've determined your ideal pie, ask yourself along the way if you are staying true to this. Is it week 3 and you are you spending 90% of your time and energy on repertoire when you determined that 40% was the most balanced and healthy for you? What needs to change – the goal or the implementation?

It can be very helpful to sit down and think about this balance in terms of all the other areas of your life as well. What matters most to you? What does your life look like when you are most content and – as a result – playing your best?

Identify the areas of your life from which you derive the most meaning, purpose, joy, and general well-being. Check in with yourself throughout your preparation – especially when feeling "stuck" – and honestly ask yourself if you are neglecting any or all of these areas of your life.

We are so much more than our playing and, as my good friend Denys Derome always says, "We play how we are." While this can mean many things, it can sometimes be most obvious in someone who has dedicated 100% of their energy to the instrument, pushing down and away every other part of their life that doesn't seemingly directly make them a better player. While it may appear as though dedicating everything to the instrument is the best way to "get ahead" in audition preparation, for most people it is not. If your life is lacking joy or physical, mental, and emotional health, it will come out in your playing, no matter how well you think you've prepared.

What matters most to YOU?

An example of this sort of brainstorming of balance can be found on the following page (fig. 4.5).

Balance Assessment: Life – Sample (figure 4.5)

Area	Important Components for Me	Am I taking care in this area?
Physical Health	regular exercise; 8-9 hours of sleep; eating clean; drinking water	my sleep is suffering lately!
Mental and Emotional Health	meditating; going for walks; speaking with my therapist/coach	great!
Social Life	spending time with friends; creating and keeping boundaries -- give myself space	I feel content!
Everyday Life	keeping up with bills and keeping my living space clean and tidy	ok...
Spiritual Life	going to church; meditation; reflection	I feel content!
Musical Life	sticking to audition plan! listening to and playing other music	good!
Creativity	creating things outside of music -- writing; painting	I would like to do this more often
Intellectual Life	reading; studying languages	haven't done Italian work in months! would like to read more

PLANNING AND PRACTICING

5

"Practice puts brains in your muscles."

Sam Snead

Plan your practice and practice your plan

The single most important part of your preparation is likely your practice. Whether you choose to practice in 2-hour sessions or 20-minute sessions, it's up to you – as long as you go in with a plan! The goal of this section of the Audition Playbook is not to teach you *how* to practice, but instead to encourage you to be deliberate and thoughtful in the planning and execution of your practice. Our time is already limited, but how many times have you thought before an audition, "If only I had just *one… more… week…*"? Every session counts.

The assessments and goals charts you have filled out so far are all there to help you better plan your day-to-day or week-to-week practice. If those assessments point to some major holes in technique or knowledge of the repertoire, you will need to adjust your practice plan to work on these areas.

However you choose to practice, have a plan in advance. Choose one night to designate every week as your planning and reflecting night. Sit down and write out what your broad practice goals are for the week. What do you wish to have accomplished by this time next week? What did you not quite finish this week? Write it all down and give yourself a rough arc for the following seven days.

You should also aim to block out ten minutes every night to reflect upon the day's work and plan out your practice for the following day. Use the data you collected today, along with your plan and goals for the week, to structure tomorrow's practice sessions.

You will not always stick to the plan – and that's okay! Remember to be flexible with yourself. The point is to *have* a plan that you are constantly evaluating and reevaluating along the way. After a few days of committing to this, you start to pick up momentum from planning and seeing your plan come to fruition.

Write it all down

Write down your plan. **Just do it.** If you plan to spend 30 minutes on Bach, don't just go into the room and *say* you're going to spend 30 minutes on Bach. Write it down in your practice journal. Write it down here, in a separate notebook, on your computer or tablet, a sticky note – whatever – **just write it down.** Writing things down is not only a contract with yourself, but documentation you can look back upon tomorrow, next week, or in three weeks to see when you last touched on something and what you worked on within that piece.

Even if you work something for only five minutes, you'll likely discover *something.* Write it down! Maybe you are working to get an excerpt up to speed – write down the tempo you left off with today. Maybe your articulation is unclear – note that for tomorrow. Maybe you realized it's easier if you think of the flute part before you come in – write that down. Maybe you're suddenly feeling really tense as you start playing this particular excerpt – write that down and find out why.

If you only take one thing from this book, let it be this – write everything down.

Planning and tracking weekly and daily goals and practice

However you choose to plan your practice – with the charts provided in the Audition Playbook or by your own method – be sure to step back and develop a big-picture outline of practice goals for the week. Remember to consider any other playing or personal obligations you have over the course of the next seven days before setting any goals a little too unattainable. If you are playing principal trumpet on Mahler 5 all week, you'll probably want to do more mental rehearsal than physical practice.

In planning your daily practice, include how much time you plan to allot to each session *and* each individual item within a session. Leave space to write down any observations you make throughout the sessions.

Sample Daily and Weekly practice plans are at the end of this chapter (figs. 5.2 and 5.3). In the Daily Practice example, please note that the timings in certain sessions are 3-5 minutes per item and 20-30 in other sessions; this is simply to show how to use the chart, not to recommend any one way of practicing over another. For this reason, the chart is very open-ended and –   for lack of a better word – vague. Use the Daily Practice chart however it best suits you.

Dividing up the repertoire list

It can get a little overwhelming when first deciding which excerpts to practice when. Always be referring back to and adjusting the Repertoire Assessment to better inform your practice plan week to week. It can also be helpful to divide up the audition repertoire list into two or three separate lists. (This is especially useful if you are preparing two audition lists at once). There are many ways you can divide up the list. I have outlined my preferred method below:

1. Go through the repertoire list and take note of the excerpts that are going to require the most focus and also the ones that are the most tiring to practice. Create a list of these excerpts.

2. Divide the list from #1 in half to ensure you do not assign all of the heavy lifting to the same day. Label these two lists A and B.

3. Go through the rest of the repertoire list and assign the remaining excerpts to the A and B lists equally.

4. Once you are happy with how the lists are divided, you can plan the week ahead. I like to have two A-days, two B-days, two C-days, and one day of rest. C-days are "catch-all" days. On these days, I either work on whatever needs most review from the previous days, work specifically on the weakest excerpts, or use it as a day of mock auditions and recording. To avoid over-practicing, injury, and burnout – and to accommodate whatever other playing obligations I have for the week – I assign primary and secondary practice days for each category. I notate this as 1 for a primary day (heavier practicing) and 2 for a secondary day (lighter practicing). On Sundays, I just do simple fundamentals and rest.

On the following page, you will find a sample week (fig. 5.1).

Sample Week of Practicing Divided by Day (figure 5.1)

Monday	A1	Heavy practicing on the A list
Tuesday	B2	Lighter practicing on the B list
Wednesday	C2	Lighter practicing on select excerpts from both lists OR mock auditions
Thursday	B1	Heavier practice on the B list
Friday	A2	Lighter practice on the A list
Saturday	C1	Heavier practice on select excerpts from both lists OR mock auditions
Sunday	rest	One hour of fundamentals; run through a few excerpts; rest

Mental practicing

As stated in Chapter 1, mental practice is a very important part of audition preparation. Because this area is especially variable and highly personal, the space provided for planning mental practice is labeled as "Mental Training" in the Weekly Practice Goals sheets. You may choose to be far more detailed and specific with your mental practice plans on a daily basis. I suggest utilizing the Daily Practice sheets for this. In the Daily Practice sample provided (fig. 5.3), mental practice sessions are labeled as MR (mental rehearsal or practicing) and MP (mental performance or visualizing a round of the audition).

Weekly Practicing Planning – Sample (figure 5.2)

Reflection on Last Week
Spent a lot of time focusing on the new-to-me excerpts. Need to return to working on fundamentals and easy playing. Felt like I overdid it. Didn't mentally practice very much.

OVERVIEW OF SCHEDULE						
Sun	Mon	Tues	Weds	Thurs	Fri	Sat
Jeff's recital	Morning rehearsal; evening pops concert	Morning rehearsal; doc appt at 8a	Off	Mahler 5 (don't practice much)	Mahler 5	Rehearsal in evening

Focus and Goals	Priorities
Lots of fundamentals this week. Focus on easy breath in, easy breath out. Tongue placement forward and flat. Start each session with centering and clear mind.	Fundamentals; weakest 3 excerpts slowly practiced; more mental practice.

Mental Preparation	Other
Two 15-minute sessions per day... one Mental Practice, one Mental Performance of easy 1st rounds	Family will be in town for Mahler so I will have a little less time to practice.

Daily Practice Planning – Sample (figure 5.3)

		Nov. 1; session 1:	5	MR: Brahms 1	
5	flexibility studies		5	MR: Till Eulenspiegel	clarity of pitches; not hearing correctly
5	brahms 2	play with a drone	5	MR: Mozart	opening up to tempo
3	low exercise		10	MP: Round 1	Mozart, Brahms 1, Till, Mahler, Heldenleben
3	tchaikovsky		5	Shostakovich	
5	etude #2	quarter = 100	5	Schoenberg	
5	mozart	record tomorrow	3	scales	
	session 2:		3	flexibility study #3	
20	mahler	get it softer	5	Bach	
20	mozart	clearer 8ths	5	etude #4	
20	mussorgsky	endurance... play this more often...	5	MR: Brahms	visualizing starting with ease
	session 3:		5	MR: Haydn	visualize practicing to increase tempo
20	etudes 3,7	slowly	5	MR: Heldenleben	visualize opening 4 bars
10	strauss	play earlier in the day tomorrow			

6

The importance of practicing performing

"Why don't I sound as good on stage as I do in the practice room?" Replicating what it feels like to perform is an important and often overlooked part of audition preparation. Nerves, mind games, the fact that you only have "one shot" – this stuff doesn't happen in the practice room. How do we perform our best under pressure when we spend most of our time alone and without an audience? By practicing under pressure again and again and creating audiences wherever possible.

The two strategies in the Audition Playbook for re-creating the performance environment and creating an audience are recordings (performing for yourself and your microphone) and mock auditions (performing for yourself and/or your friends).

Recording yourself

We all know that we need to record. It's up to you how and when to record. You may want to record every practice session, or one per day, or two per week. You may want to record a "mock round" every day. It's up to you. Recording will not only highlight tempo and intonation discrepancies that you might be unaware of, but by pressing the red record button, you are turning up the heat, ever so slightly, and recreating physical and mental sensations of live performance.

When listening back to your recordings, utilize the Recording Assessments chart (sample below) to listen for discrepancies of pitch, timing, sound, clarity, and musical picture. How does the tape match what you thought you were doing?

What is different about "performing" for the microphone versus just running through the excerpts at the end of the day?

Mock auditions

Playing for real human beings is important too. Take time to seriously consider what will make mock auditions the most beneficial for you. How many people should you play for? Who should you play for? How often? When? Where? Do you want comments every time? Everyone is different, but generally it is not helpful to load up and collect as many opinions as possible. Set a limit for yourself. Stop playing for people – at least for comments – between one to two weeks out from the audition date. Lastly, stick to people who will be honest but supportive and positive.

And don't wait too long to plan this! Too many times we tell ourselves we're going to do a ton of mock auditions leading up to the big day and then never get them off the ground. Plan these in advance. At the very least, write a date in your calendar. Try to reserve different spaces with different acoustics. Ask the people you'd like to play for well in advance and be clear with your panel about what you're hoping to gain. If you want them to throw curveballs and distractions your way, let them know. If you want nothing more than warm bodies in the room and no comments coming your way, tell them. Record your mocks and write reflections on what happens. To sum it up, pick a date, reserve a space, invite some people, record, and reflect!

On the following page, you will find samples of the Mock Audition Planning and Reflections charts (figs. 6.2 and 6.3), as well as the Recording Reflection Chart (fig. 6.1).

Recording Reflection – Sample (figure 6.1)

Piece	Rhythm	Intonation	Clarity / Sound	Musical Picture & Notes
Mozart 2	slow coming off long notes; rushing at 27	occasionally written D's sound high... usually when descending	sound is very clear; articulation can be a little clearer	can be lighter and happier sounding; I feel I tensed up a bit more because I was recording
Shostakovich	very solid	a few wobbly notes	uneven in the middle when crossing ranges	very solid
Beethoven 6	rushing a tiny bit	good	good	can relax a bit! feel centered and grounded before starting!

Mock Audition: Planning – Sample (figure 6.2)

Date	Audience	Location	Notes	confirmed?
11/14	Peter, Paul, and Mary	Tanna Hall	Mary will read through concerto with me on piano	yes
11/22	Jerry, Morty, Summer	P-242	no feedback	waiting to hear back on the room

Mock Audition: Reflection – Sample (figure 6.3)

Date	My thoughts	Audience feedback	What I hear on the recording
11/14	Felt very nervous and my focus was on how shaky I felt and must have seen to the audience	They thought I was very centered and poised, despite how I felt inside. Loud stuff can be a little softer. Rhythm and intonation are both very good.	I don't sound as nervous as I felt; Mozart can be a lot lighter; Mahler is very impressive; more accurate than I thought
11/22	Felt like I played at 90% of my potential. Overall very strong.	I asked for no feedback	Very strong round; can still play the loud excerpts a little less.

SCENARIO PLANNING

7

What could possibly go wrong?

Things happen. You can plan and plan and plan but life can change on a dime. Under the pressure of an audition, even the smallest surprises can feel huge. Accepting that things can and will go wrong and having some sort of contingency plan and/or mantra for handling it can have a huge impact on your ability to bounce back and not let the surprises affect your performances.

Plan in advance when you will walk to the hall, how you will get there, etc. Whenever possible, rehearse the walk to the hall the day before the audition (and plan for this rehearsal walk). Plan what you will eat and when. Mentally rehearse all of the important details as the day gets closer. Also, brainstorm the more "what-if" scenarios... what if your flight is delayed? What if a string breaks before you go on? What if you are rushed into the next round? What if they ask you to play something not on the list?

Brainstorming scenarios and reactions is not to worry you, nor is it meant for you to obsess over. However, when something goes wrong, there can be great comfort in knowing you've already considered this possibility and your response. In most cases, just having a planned mindset for your reaction to surprises can be powerful enough. A great mantra to have and rehearse for the unplanned, unpredicted, and unwanted is simply, "I'll handle it." Pause. Breathe. "I'll handle it." And then handle it!

What else might they ask?

Many audition lists include the possibility of sight-reading. I like to take a look at the list and ask myself if there are any big pieces suspiciously missing from the list that might show up in a later or section playing round. For example, if it's a fourth horn audition without Beethoven 9 – the biggest fourth horn solo in the repertoire – I'd take note of that and make sure I had it in my back pocket just in case. I have taken auditions where the "sight-reading" pieces in the finals were in fact standard solos not on the list. Knowing this was a possibility, it did not throw me off, even if I did not work on those pieces leading up to the audition.

With section jobs, I also like to take note of which pieces on the list – and even some others not on the list – could possibly be for the section round. I will take time to play through these excerpts both with friends and recordings. Additionally, if this orchestra is "known" for a certain piece being on auditions or being played by them, it's worth taking a look at as well.

Of course, you can't prepare the entire catalogue of repertoire for your instrument. Don't get bogged down by this. If sight-reading is an overwhelming concern for you, it's not the repertoire that needs your attention – it's the skill of sight-reading. Set aside a short session every day or two to practice sight-reading short pieces and études and work to develop a sight-reading mental routine.

Writing your script

In addition to accounting for the possible surprises of the audition itself, in the Audition Day Script you will plan out all of your logistics – travel, accommodations, warm-up plan, what you'll eat, etc. It's a good idea to start working on this as early as possible and mentally rehearse the different aspects of it. By audition day, it will be a breeze, as you will have already done all of this many times – in your head. There is space in your script to add anything else you think is pertinent.

After the audition

Win or lose, if you learn even *one* thing during this audition process, it will have been a success and a big step towards winning the next. What worked? What didn't work? What surprised you? Which excerpts remained worrisome throughout preparation and/or suddenly felt uneasy on audition day? Write it all down – as soon as possible – and before the mandatory post-audition libations.

Even if it's just on a cocktail napkin or a note on your phone to later write in your Playbook, it is very important to reflect upon your audition while it is still fresh in your mind. If you wait a few days, you can lose some of the most important details of the experience. Your memory of the audition becomes whatever *stories* of the audition you told your friends at the bar or your mother on the phone afterwards! Sometimes those re-tellings are embellished, even unintentionally, with certain details omitted or changed. This is only natural but it does not help you in moving forward. Write down those thoughts and feelings as soon as possible. This information will be extremely valuable in the preparation of your next audition – whether that's in ten days or ten years.

And then, of course, celebrate!

On the following pages, you will find sample charts from the Audition Day Script.

Audition Day Script: Things That Can Go Wrong – Sample (figure 7.1)

Scenario	Reaction
I don't sleep well the night before	I expected this so I can't let it bother me. I will let myself sleep in as much as possible without making me rush.
I forgot to bring enough food	I'll ask if they have any snacks or to step out for a moment
I am being rushed by the proctor	
My car breaks down	

Audition Day Script: Additional Possible Repertoire – Sample (figure 7.2)

Section Round	Possible Sight Reading
Beethoven 3	Beethoven 9 – 4th horn solo
Dvorak Cello Concerto	Don Quixote (was on the list last time)
Der Freischutz	Tchaikovsky 5 (was sight reading last time)

Audition Day Script – Sample (figure 7.3)

Audition date: Tuesday, Dec 5	Playing Time: Report at 10a; number draw at 10:30
Travel plans: Flying Sun, Dec 3; landing at 4pm; Uber to hotel; arrive around 6p	Accommodations: Waterfront Hotel close to hall
Day before: Sleep in until 9am; warm up; practice a little in the morning; scope out the walk to the hall; watch tv; center often	Night before: In bed by 10p; have everything packed and start night time routine at 9p
Things to bring: Black bag; food; mute; water; music; iPad; headphones;	What to eat and when: 8am clif bar; 9am banana; pack sandwich for lunch and almonds
Departure and arrival times on audition day: Leave hotel at 9:30a (15min walk); arrive at 9:45	Warm-up time: 9am at hotel; 10a warm up a little bit at hall
Personal warm-up room plan: 1. center; 2. warm up 5 minutes; 3. visualize starting each excerpt; 4 practice starting each excerpt; 5. stretch	Group warm-up room plan: Headphones on and buzz; do not play much at all.
Plan between rounds: Read my book; determine how much down time I have; listen to podcasts; buzz	what to do if my car breaks down or my logistics don't go as planned: take a breath and remind myself "I can handle this!" – call the personnel manager if I am running behind. It will be ok. I can handle this!

FINAL THOUGHTS

Throughout your Audition Playbook journey, I hope you will reach out and share your experiences, feedback, questions, and more.

There is a growing community of supportive Audition Playbook readers sharing their stories online. Please join the official discussion group at www.facebook.com/groups/auditionplaybook/

Keep an eye out for new articles, Audition Playbook tools, and new resources at www.auditionplaybook.com. As this is an ongoing project of learning and discovery, new materials are posted often. Your feedback and conversations help keep the project evolving! Additionally, PDF downloads of certain worksheets from the book are available on the website as well as digital downloads and updated versions of the tools in the book.

Please feel free to contact me directly through the website at www.auditionplaybook.com/contact/

Lastly, please follow @auditionplaybook on Facebook and Instagram.

ACKNOWLEDGEMENTS

Thank you first and foremost to Andrew Bain for teaching me so much about the horn, auditioning, and performing over the past few years and for encouraging the development of this book. I can never repay you for your kindness, encouragement, generosity, and – maybe especially – your patience. I am so grateful for all you've given me.

Thank you to Dr. Don Greene for teaching me how to audition, train, and think, and for being so supportive and generous in the development of this book.

Thank you to my dear friend and mentor Denys Derome for all you've taught me – and sometimes taught me repeatedly until it finally stuck – both on the horn and off.

Thank you to Michael Winter for your audition masterclass at Tanglewood, which inspired the development of the Four Phases of Preparation and to Dr. Nate Zeisler for all of your guidance in getting this project off the ground. Thank you also to my many friends, colleagues, and mentors who have looked over the material, tried things out, asked questions, and offered their feedback and encouragement in the initial stages. You are all wonderful.

Thank you to my family, who instilled in my the entrepreneurial spirit and desire to work hard. I love you.

And lastly, thank you to the many Audition Playbook readers and supporters who have kept in touch, shared their experiences and feedback, asked questions, and given insights. Please continue to keep in touch and keep the conversations going! Your support and feedback has been monumental in keeping this project going.

RESOURCES

Mental Training

Afremow, Jim. *The Champion's Mind*. Rodale, 2015.

Greene, Don. *Audition Success*. Routledge, 2002.

Greene, Don. *Fight Your Fear and Win: 7 Skills for Performing Your Best Under Pressure*. Broadway Books, 2002.

Greene, Don. *Performance Success: Performing Your Best Under Pressure*. Routledge, 2017.

Greene, Don. *Winning on Stage*, 2019, www.winningonstage.com/.

Mack, Gary, and David Casstevens. *Mind Gym: An Athlete's Guide to Inner Excellence*. McGraw-Hill, 2007.

Mumford, George. *The Mindful Athlete: Secrets to Pure Performance*. Parallax Press, 2016.

Rotella, Robert J., and Robert Cullen. *Golf Is Not a Game of Perfect*. Simon & Schuster, 2004.

Selk, Jason. *10-Minute Toughness: The Mental Exercise Program for Winning Before the Game Begins*. McGraw-Hill, 2009.

Balance, Health, and Wellness

Brown Brené. *The Power of Vulnerability Teachings on Authenticity, Connection, and Courage.* Sounds True, 2012.

De Alcantara, Pedro. *Indirect Procedures A Musician's Guide to the Alexander Technique.* Oxford University Press, 2013.

Epstein, Mark. *Going to Pieces without Falling Apart: a Buddhist Perspective on Wholeness.* Thorsons, 1999.

Harris, Dan. *10% Happier: How I Tamed the Voice in My Head, Reduced Stress without Losing My Edge, and Found Self-Help That Actually Works: a True Story.* Yellow Kite, 2019.

Horvath, Janet. *Playing (Less) Hurt: an Injury Prevention Guide for Musicians.* Hal Leonard Books, 2010.

Kabat-Zinn, Jon. *Wherever You Go, There You Are.* Piatkus, 2004.

Kleinman, Judith, and Peter Buckoke. *The Alexander Technique for Musicians.* Methuen Drama, 2018.

Klickstein, Gerald. *The Musician's Way: a Guide to Practice, Performance, and Wellness.* Oxford University Press, 2009.

Morton, Jennie. *The Authentic Performer: Wearing a Mask and the Effect on Health.* Compton Publishing, 2015.

Salzberg, Sharon. *Real Happiness: the Power of Meditation: a 28-Day Program.* Workman Pub., 2010.

Zander, Lauren Handel. *Maybe It's You: Cut the Crap. Face Your Fears. Love Your Life.* Hachette Books, 2018.

Goal-Setting and Productivity

Allen, David. *Getting Things Done: the Art of Stress-Free Productivity*. Piatkus,
2019.

Elrod, Hal. *The Miracle Morning: Key Takeaways, Analysis and Review*.
Eureka Books, 2012.

"A Simple Way to Break a Bad Habit." Judson Brewer, TED,
www.ted.com/talks/
judson_brewer_a_simple_way_to_break_a_bad_habit.

Tracy, Brian. *Eat That Frog!: 21 Great Ways to Stop Procrastinating and Get
More Done in Less Time*. Berrett-Koehler Publishers, Inc, 2017.

Audition Preparation

Hawley, Richie. "Your Next Audition." Richie Hawley,
www.richiehawley.com/artist.php?view=news&nid=1544.

Jenkins, Rachelle. "Interview with Andrew Bain, Principal Horn of the LA Phil,
on Auditions, Practicing, and the Importance of the Process." Audition
Playbook, 23 July 2018, www.auditionplaybook.com/blog/bain-
interview.

Jenkins, Rachelle. "Taking the Honesty Pill: An Interview with Christopher Still,
2nd Trumpet of the LA Phil." Audition Playbook, 16 May 2019,
www.auditionplaybook.com/blog/still-honesty-pill.

Jenkins, Rachelle. "The Four Pillars of Audition Preparation." Audition

Playbook, 25 Aug. 2018, www.auditionplaybook.com/blog/four-
pillars.

Montone, Jen. "Sample Audition Preparation Plan." Jen Montone,

www.jenmontone.com/sample-audition/.

Nuccio, Mark. "Orchestral Preparation in 10 Steps." Audition Cafe, 26 June

2017, auditioncafe.com/article/orchestral-preparation-in-10-steps/.

Oft, Toby. "Articles." Toby Oft, www.tobyoft.com/articles/.

Taylor, Brant. "10 Tips for a Successful Orchestral Audition." The Strad, 15 Feb.

2017, www.thestrad.com/10-tips-for-a-successful-orchestral-audition/
14.article.

Practice Tools

Bosler, Annie, and Don Greene. "How to Practice Effectively...for Just about

Anything." TED, TED-Ed, ed.ted.com/lessons/how-to-practice-
effectively-for-just-about-anything-annie-bosler-and-don-greene.

Jenkins, Rachelle. "Favorite Practice Apps of 2019." Audition Playbook, 14

Mar. 2019, www.auditionplaybook.com/blog/2019/3/13/favorite-
practice-apps-of-2019.

Jenkins, Rachelle. "How to Create Spliced Recordings of Your Excerpts."

Audition Playbook, 19 Mar. 2019, www.auditionplaybook.com/blog/
how-to-create-spliced-recordings-of-your-excerpts-7cslp.

Oft, Toby. "Practice and the Law of Diminishing Returns." Toby Oft,

www.tobyoft.com/practice-and-the-law-of-diminishing-returns.

Art, Creativity, and Musical Ideas

Cameron, Julia. *The Artist's Way: a Spiritual Path to Higher Creativity*. Pan,
1995.

Frederiksen, Brian, and John Taylor. *Arnold Jacobs: Song and Wind.*
WindSong Press, 2006.

McGill, David. *Sound in Motion: a Performer's Guide to Greater Musical
Expression.* Indiana Univ. Press, 2007.

Pressfield, Steven. *The War of Art: Winning the Inner Creative Battle.* Rugged
Land, 2002.

Zander, Rosamund Stone. *Art of Possibility: Transforming Professional and
Personal Life.* Harvard Business Review Press, 2014.

AUDITION PLAYBOOK

OPTIMAL PLANNING FOR ORCHESTRAL AUDITION SUCCESS

Part Two: The Workbook

AUDITION PLAYBOOK

AUDITION:______________________

DATE OF AUDITION:__________

PHASES OF PREPARATION: WEEKLY PLANS

DATE OF AUDITION:
WEEKS UNTIL AUDITION:

(circle one)	**PLANNING**	**EARLY**	**CORE**	**POCKET**
6 week plan	week 6 (2-3 days)	week 6 (4-5 days)	weeks 5, 4, 3, first half of 2 (3.5 weeks)	weeks 2, 1 (1.5 weeks)
5 week plan	week 5 (2 days)	week 5 (5 days)	weeks 4, 3, 2	week 1
4 week plan	week 4 (2 days)	week 4 (5 days)	weeks 4, 3, 2	week 1
custom				
(on the line below, write out the dates you will spend in each phase, based on the plan you have chosen):				
dates:				

PHASES OF PREPARATION:
CHECKLIST

PLANNING

dates:

	Résumé is submitted; participation confirmed; deposit sent.
	Mark up calendar — how many weeks? Choose phase plan and assign dates to each phase.
	Fill out Goals sheet. Brainstorm preparation and performance goals.
	Create playlists of the audition repertoire.
	Prepare the excerpt book:
	Print and bind; mark the excerpts.
	Mark tempi and translations.
	Start writing technical & character lists for each excerpt. Why is this on the list and what will I showcase?
	Start gathering your "happy-place" materials — motivating, calming books/podcasts/movies.
	Commit to planning practice every day.
	Get into the habit of Airplane Mode for all practice and preparation sessions.
	Develop a pre-practice routine of centering, stretching, breathing — setting yourself up for an easy, efficient session — every day.

EARLY PREPARATION

dates:

	Play through the list and make a preliminary recording of each excerpt to establish your baseline.
	Decide how to best divide the repertoire list.
	Fill out the Repertoire Assessment — check back in often!
	Fill out the Technique Assessment.
	Determine which excerpts will need the most focus — the "everyday" excerpts.
	Complete your technical/character lists.
	Fill out Additional Possible Rep list.
	Start listening to your repertoire playlists daily, focusing on the character and getting in that headspace. Practice mentally snapping into that character.
	Reserve rooms/dates/people for mock auditions.
	Reserve rooms/dates/people to play with pianists.
	Fill out the Possible Additional Repertoire list — print and listen to these pieces.
	Make travel and accommodation plans.
	Fill out Balance charts. Start paying more attention to your eating and sleeping habits.
	Get into the habit of centering as you would in performance before each practice session. Start ironing out mental routines.
	Focus most of your attention on building technique and mental picture — work on the weaknesses that could eliminate you.
	Work on things slowly and establish a default setting of ease and efficiency.
	Start working on your Audition Day Script.

dates:

	Start and end each day with breathing, stretching, centering to get in the zone.
	Eat, sleep, and treat your mind and body as though you're training for the Olympics — without overdoing it. Listen to your body.
	Keep checking in with your Goals and Balance sheets — adjust accordingly.
	Keep checking in and adjusting your Repertoire Assessment and listening to the recordings daily.
	Always be working, reviewing, and mentally rehearsing your Audition Day Script.
	Always be using metronome and drones. Start and end each day with the drone to relax your pitch.
	Decide how often to play for people (and whom) and whether or not to receive comments. Record each time and reflect.
	Record your practice as much as possible while still beneficial — don't get bogged down by or negative about this.
	Train yourself to play any excerpt at any time and in any condition — enlist your friends to challenge you.
	Keep playing and listening to music you enjoy that's not on the list.
	Surround yourself with positivity — supportive and positive people, media, etc. Enforce and/or create your boundaries!
	Play genuinely. If it sounds contrived, it is.
	Google image search the hall and start visualizing yourself playing there.
	Record yourself in different halls with the mic in different spots.
	Rehearse the solo with pianists — without rehearsal, as it will likely be in the audition.
	Sort out any final logistics.

dates:

	Find your happy place and stay there. Eliminate anything stressful for the next week — the news, social media, difficult conversations and people, and stressful tv shows. Embrace what you love.
	Continue to follow your pre-practice routines — don't change anything now for a big surprise on audition day.
	Taper your daily practice — the hard work is done. More mental rehearsal and easy fundamentals, less drilling the excerpts.
	Exercise, get outside, and breathe. Just don't overdo it.
	Read and relax. Take your mind off of things but don't sloth.
	Review your (now completed) Audition Day Script. Keep mentally rehearsing this plan.
	Drink lots of water — stay hydrated! Eat good foods that make you feel your best.
	Significantly limit playing for people. Only play for those you know will be supportive and boost your confidence. You don't need comments at this point.
	Stay surrounded by positive people and enjoy exercising those boundaries you've created — it's liberating!
	Finalize your packing, food, and to-do lists and any last minute travel plans. Wrap up any and all loose ends.
	Keep your GOAL in mind — nothing else matters!
	Remind yourself that you're in the home stretch. Nothing significant will be fixed in the next week. Trust yourself and the work you've put in and enjoy this time.
	AFTER THE AUDITION
	Write your reflection.
	Reward yourself!

AUDITION GOALS

<table>
<tr><td align="center">Past Auditions Reflection</td></tr>
<tr><td>

</td></tr>
<tr><td align="center">Goals for Preparation</td></tr>
<tr><td>

</td></tr>
</table>

AUDITION GOALS, CONT'D

Audition Day Goals

Other Goals

INITIAL TECHNIQUE ASSESSMENT

Technique	Assessment	Spotlight Excerpts	Ways to Improve

Technique	Assessment	Spotlight Excerpts	Ways to Improve

ALTERNATE TECHNIQUE ASSESSMENT

Parts of my technique that are shaky and could eliminate me	Parts of my technique that are pretty solid and reliable	Parts of my technique that are really special and will set me apart from the rest

Parts of my technique that are shaky and could eliminate me	Parts of my technique that are pretty solid and reliable	Parts of my technique that are really special and will set me apart from the rest

REPERTOIRE ASSESSMENT

TODAY'S DATE:
AUDITION DATE:

Piece	1	2	3	Technical & Musical Factors

REPERTOIRE ASSESSMENT, CONT'D

Piece	1	2	3	Technical & Musical Factors

BALANCE ASSESSMENT: PREPARATION

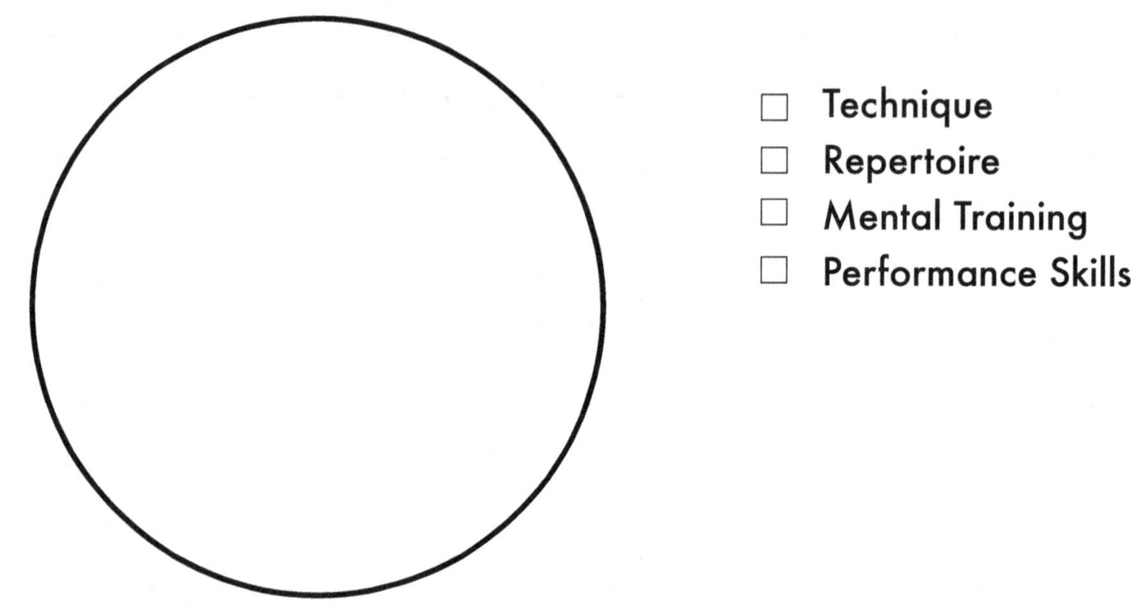

- ☐ Technique
- ☐ Repertoire
- ☐ Mental Training
- ☐ Performance Skills

WHAT DOES BALANCED PREPARATION MEAN TO ME?
HOW SHOULD I BEST DIVIDE & PRIORITIZE MY TIME?

BALANCE ASSESSMENT: LIFE

Area	Important components for me	Am I taking care in this area?

WEEKLY PRACTICE PLAN

date:

week: 8   7   6   5   4   3   2   1

Reflection on Last Week

OVERVIEW OF SCHEDULE						
Sun	Mon	Tues	Weds	Thurs	Fri	Sat

Focus and Goals	Priorities

Mental Preparation	Other

DAILY PRACTICE PLAN

date:

focus and priorities:

DAILY PRACTICE PLAN

date:	
focus and priorities:	

DAILY PRACTICE PLAN

date:
focus and priorities:

DAILY PRACTICE PLAN

date:

focus and priorities:

DAILY PRACTICE PLAN

date:

focus and priorities:

DAILY PRACTICE PLAN

date:		
focus and priorities:		

DAILY PRACTICE PLAN

date:

focus and priorities:

WEEKLY PRACTICE PLAN

date:

week: 8   7   6   5   4   3   2   1

Reflection on Last Week

OVERVIEW OF SCHEDULE						
Sun	Mon	Tues	Weds	Thurs	Fri	Sat

Focus and Goals	Priorities
Mental Preparation	Other

DAILY PRACTICE PLAN

date:

focus and priorities:

DAILY PRACTICE PLAN

date:		
focus and priorities:		

DAILY PRACTICE PLAN

date:

focus and priorities:

DAILY PRACTICE PLAN

date:

focus and priorities:

DAILY PRACTICE PLAN

date:	
focus and priorities:	

DAILY PRACTICE PLAN

date:	
focus and priorities:	

DAILY PRACTICE PLAN

date:

focus and priorities:

WEEKLY PRACTICE PLAN

date:

week: 8 7 6 5 4 3 2 1

Reflection on Last Week

OVERVIEW OF SCHEDULE						
Sun	Mon	Tues	Weds	Thurs	Fri	Sat

Focus and Goals	Priorities

Mental Preparation	Other

DAILY PRACTICE PLAN

date:		
focus and priorities:		

DAILY PRACTICE PLAN

date:

focus and priorities:

DAILY PRACTICE PLAN

date:

focus and priorities:

DAILY PRACTICE PLAN

date:

focus and priorities:

DAILY PRACTICE PLAN

date:	
focus and priorities:	

DAILY PRACTICE PLAN

date:		
focus and priorities:		

DAILY PRACTICE PLAN

date:

focus and priorities:

WEEKLY PRACTICE PLAN

date:

week: 8 7 6 5 4 3 2 1

Reflection on Last Week

OVERVIEW OF SCHEDULE						
Sun	Mon	Tues	Weds	Thurs	Fri	Sat

Focus and Goals	Priorities
Mental Preparation	Other

DAILY PRACTICE PLAN

date:		
focus and priorities:		

DAILY PRACTICE PLAN

date:

focus and priorities:

DAILY PRACTICE PLAN

date:

focus and priorities:

DAILY PRACTICE PLAN

date:		
focus and priorities:		

DAILY PRACTICE PLAN

date:	
focus and priorities:	

DAILY PRACTICE PLAN

date:		
focus and priorities:		

DAILY PRACTICE PLAN

date:		
focus and priorities:		

RECORDINGS ASSESSMENTS

PIECE	RHYTHM	INTONATION	CLARITY OF SOUND & MUSICAL PICTURE

RECORDINGS ASSESSMENTS, CONT'D

PIECE	RHYTHM	INTONATION	CLARITY OF SOUND & MUSICAL PICTURE

MOCK AUDITION PLANNING

DATE	AUDIENCE	LOCATION	NOTES	CONFIRMED?

MOCK AUDITION REFLECTIONS

DATE	MY THOUGHTS	AUDIENCE FEEDBACK	WHAT I HEAR ON THE RECORDING

AUDITION DAY SCRIPT:
THINGS THAT COULD GO WRONG

SCENARIO	MY PLANNED POSSIBLE REACTION

AUDITION DAY SCRIPT:
POSSIBLE ADDITIONAL REPERTOIRE

SECTION PLAYING	POSSIBLE SIGHTREADING

AUDITION DAY SCRIPT

Audition date(s):	Assigned playing time(s):
Travel plans:	Accommodations:
Things to pack for the trip:	Things to pack for the day:
Plan for day before:	Plan for night before:
Bed time before audition:	Wake-up time:
What to eat and when:	Departure & arrival times for audition day:

AUDITION DAY SCRIPT, CONT'D

Warm-up time:	Warm-up at accommodations or hall?
Plan for group warm-up waiting rooms:	Plan for personal practice room time:
Plan for down-time between rounds:	Plan for being rushed along:

POST-AUDITION REFLECTION

<table>
<tr><td align="center">WHAT WENT WELL?</td></tr>
<tr><td>

</td></tr>
<tr><td align="center">WHAT NEEDS TO IMPROVE?</td></tr>
<tr><td>

</td></tr>
</table>